The Little Book of More Calm Colouring

Portable Relaxation

David Sinden & Victoria Kay

D1494180

First published 2016 by Bluebird
an imprint of Pan Macmillan
The Smithson, 6 Briset Street, London EC1M 5NR
Associated companies throughout the world
www.panmacmillan.com

ISBN 978-1-5098-2086-3

Copyright © David Sinden and Victoria Kay 2016

The right of David Sinden and Victoria Kay to be identified as the authors and illustrators of this work has been asserted by them in accordance with the Copyright, Designs and Patents Act 1988.

All rights reserved. No part of this publication may be reproduced, stored in a retrieval system, or transmitted, in any form, or by any means (electronic, mechanical, photocopying, recording or otherwise) without the prior written permission of the publisher.

10

A CIP catalogue record for this book is available from the British Library.

Printed and bound in Italy by Printer Trento S.r.l.

This book is sold subject to the condition that it shall not, by way of trade or otherwise, be lent, hired out, or otherwise circulated without the publisher's prior consent in any form of binding or cover other than that in which it is published and without a similar condition including this condition being imposed on the subsequent purchaser.

The authors wish to thank Claire Gatzen for her help with the quotations.

This book is dedicated to Robert and Anne.

Visit **www.panmacmillan.com** to read more about all our books and to buy them. You will also find features, author interviews and news of any author events, and you can sign up for e-newsletters so that you're always first to hear about our new releases.

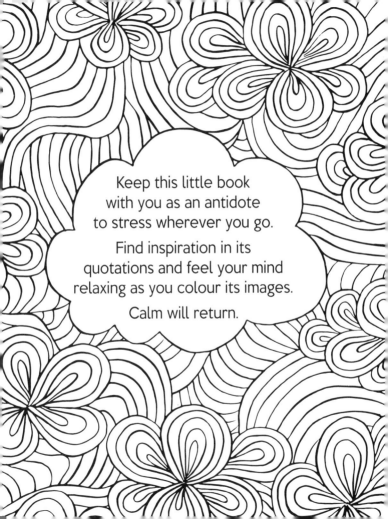

Keep this little book
with you as an antidote
to stress wherever you go.

Find inspiration in its
quotations and feel your mind
relaxing as you colour its images.

Calm will return.

Remember when life's path is steep to keep your mind even.

HORACE

A well-spent day brings happy sleep.

Leonardo da Vinci

The past, the present and the future are really one: they are today.

HARRIET BEECHER STOWE

Let the beauty of what you love
be what you do.

RUMI

One joy scatters a hundred griefs.

CHINESE PROVERB

There is nothing permanent
except change.

HERACLITUS

It is always the simple that produces the marvellous.

Amelia Barr

The idea of calm exists in a
sitting cat.

JULES RENARD

Be happy for this moment.
This moment is your life.

Omar Khayyám

Let us follow our destiny,
ebb and flow.

Virgil

Smooth seas do not make skilful sailors.

AFRICAN PROVERB

Very often it happens that a
discovery is made whilst working
upon quite another problem.

THOMAS EDISON

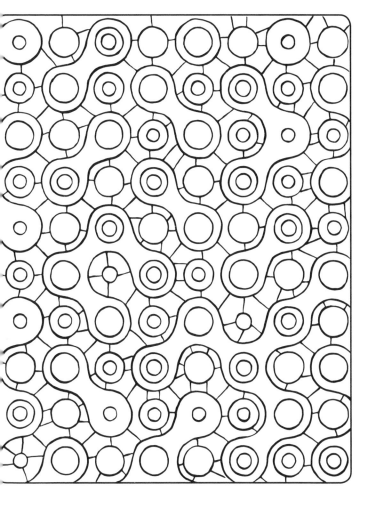

We think in eternity, but we move slowly through time.

OSCAR WILDE

Beauty is everywhere a welcome guest.

JOHANN WOLFGANG VON GOETHE

An early-morning walk is a
blessing for the whole day.

HENRY DAVID THOREAU

There is nothing like staying at home for real comfort.

JANE AUSTEN

We must cultivate our own garden.

VOLTAIRE

Life is a progress, and not a station.

Ralph Waldo Emerson

Energy rightly applied and
directed will accomplish
anything.

NELLIE BLY

That it will never come again is
what makes life so sweet.

EMILY DICKINSON

Genius is patience.

ISAAC NEWTON

Who seeks shall find.

SOPHOCLES

Happiness never decreases by being shared.

BUDDHA

Life must be lived as play.

PLATO

He who plants kindness gathers
love.

SAINT BASIL THE GREAT

Let reality be reality. Let things flow naturally forwards in whatever way they like.

LAO TZU

Turn your face to the sun and
the shadows fall behind you.

MAORI PROVERB

Of the blessings set before you make your choice, and be content.

SAMUEL JOHNSON

Greater happiness comes with simplicity than with complexity.

BUDDHA

The only journey is the one within.

RAINER MARIA RILKE

Let your hook be always cast.
In the pool where you least
expect it, will be fish.

Ovid

Less is more.

ROBERT BROWNING

To begin, begin.

WILLIAM WORDSWORTH

At the centre of your being you have the answer.

Lao Tzu

Nothing is worth more than this day.

JOHANN WOLFGANG VON GOETHE

The pursuit, even of the best things, ought to be calm and tranquil.

MARCUS TULLIUS CICERO

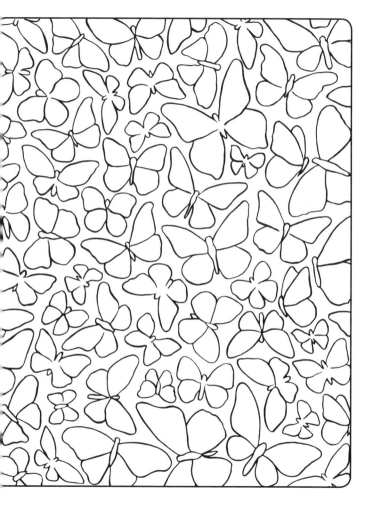

What does not destroy me,
makes me stronger.

FRIEDRICH NIETZSCHE

Forever is composed of nows.

EMILY DICKINSON

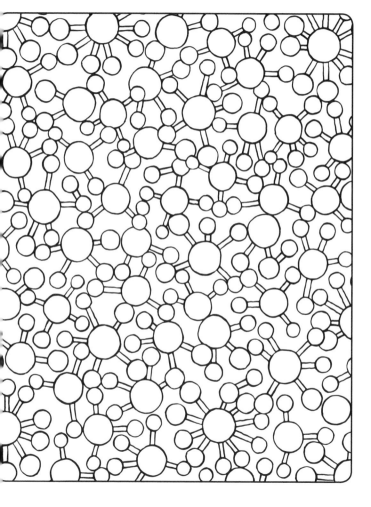

In all things of nature there is
something of the marvellous.

ARISTOTLE

I am content with what I have,
little be it or much.

JOHN BUNYAN

Everything suggests a beyond.

ISABELLA BIRD

There is geometry in the humming of the strings, there is music in the spacing of the spheres.

PYTHAGORAS

No great thing is created
suddenly.

EPICTETUS

Kites rise against, not with, the wind.

John Neal

Happiness is not an ideal of reason, but of imagination.

IMMANUEL KANT

Art has a harmony which
parallels that of nature.

PAUL CÉZANNE

Have patience and endure.

OVID

Mix a little foolishness with your serious plans.

Horace

Perfection is attained by slow degrees; it requires the hand of time.

VOLTAIRE

Have a mind that is open to everything, and attached to nothing.

TILOPA

There are those who give with joy, and that joy is their reward.

Kahlil Gibran

Nature always wears the colours
of the spirit.

RALPH WALDO EMERSON

The real voyage of discovery consists not in seeking new landscapes, but in having new eyes.

MARCEL PROUST

There is no harm in repeating a good thing.

PLATO

Nothing is impossible to a willing heart.

JOHN HEYWOOD

It is very simple to be happy but
it is very difficult to be simple.

RABINDRANATH TAGORE

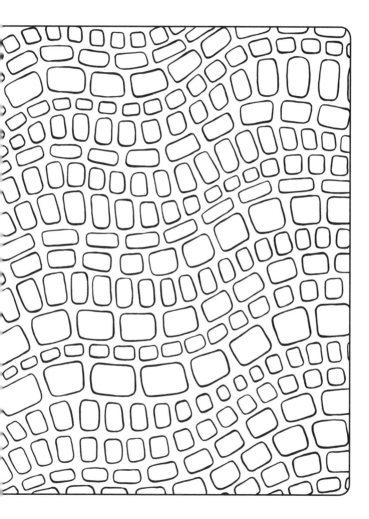

Slow and steady wins the race.

AESOP

Those who bring sunshine into the lives of others cannot keep it from themselves.

J. M. BARRIE

Against the assault of laughter
nothing can stand.

MARK TWAIN

If I keep a green bough in my heart, the singing bird will come.

CHINESE PROVERB

In every living thing there is the desire for love.

D. H. LAWRENCE

Out beyond ideas of wrongdoing
and rightdoing there is a field.
I'll meet you there.

RUMI

ALSO AVAILABLE:
The Little Book of Calm Colouring
by David Sinden & Victoria Kay

Say hello to Bluebird

Bluebird publish inspirational lifestyle books, bringing you the very latest in diet, self-help and popular psychology, as well as parenting, career and business and memoir.

We make books for life in every sense: life-enhancing but also lasting; the ones you will turn to again and again for inspiration.

Find out more about the exciting books we have coming soon:
www.bluebirdbooksforlife.com

Follow the Bluebird team on Twitter **@booksbybluebird**
We'd love to hear about your favourite **#booksforlife**

bluebird
books for life